The Boy Who Loved the Moon

Also by Thérèse Corfiatis and published by Ginninderra Press
Seasons of the Soul (with Anne Landers)
Emissaries of Light
Northern Lights

Thérèse Corfiatis

The Boy Who Loved the Moon

Acknowledgements

There are many people who played a part in this story, and I thank them for their love and belief in a little boy who deserved better. I cannot name them all, but they know who they are. How fine he has become! There are many people who still walk the road with him; I thank them also.

I thank my husband, Philip, and my son Joe, my mother, Beverley, and brothers and sisters for their ongoing support.
Our bond as a family has been strengthened by adversity.
May it continue to strengthen, no matter what life throws at us over the years to come.

A heartfelt thanks to Fay Forbes for her ever-constant patronage and encouragement.

This book is dedicated to Rose Stephens.
As a seeker of justice, and in giving a voice to those who were vulnerable in our communities, the cultivation of the seeds of my story were inspired. The seeds were there, but Rose helped water them!

The Boy Who Loved the Moon
ISBN 978 1 74027 778 5
Copyright © text Thérèse Corfiatis 2012
Cover photo: Nicholas Higgins

First published 2012
Reprinted 2019

GINNINDERRA PRESS
PO Box 3461 Port Adelaide 5015
www.ginninderrapress.com.au

Contents

The Boy Who Loved the Moon	7
Ten Fingers, Ten Toes	8
Female Intuition	10
Calamity or Care	12
Little Buddha	13
Corrugated Iron	15
At Fifteen Months	17
Baby Number Two	19
To Play, or How Not to Play	20
A Son Foretold	22
Sideways Glancing	24
Little Arms Held Up	26
Wait and See	28
Strange New World	30
A Pyramid of Three	32
Pressure Builds	34
Other People	35
Monologue of the Self	37
Irrational Fears	39
Irrational Loves	42
Rational Loves	45
Thinking in New Ways	47
Forward Planning	49
Stress Gains Momentum	51
Teasing and Tantrums	54
Collision Course	56
Burnt at the Stake	57
Five is a Magical Number	58
Taking it to the Next Level	60
Suffer the Little Children	62

Looking For Justice	63
Marvellous Marion Primary School	65
Legal Matters	66
No More Empty Words	68
The Hearing	70
Explorations	73
New Beginnings	75
Hope Renewed	77
Galactic Movements	78
Continuum	80
Autist – Moon Searcher	81

The Boy Who Loved the Moon

The mother held her son beneath the stars,
Jacaranda trees so beautiful in bloom
His little face turned upwards to the sky
As she sang a song about the moon.

Ten Fingers, Ten Toes

It wasn't meant to be this way!
Ten days overdue;
hypertension;
induced labour.
Long hours of painful contractions
(she remembered how cold her feet were),
a failed epidural, foetal distress.

A rush to the operating theatre
and afterwards in recovery
a hazy recollection
of a perspex see-through crib
reaching out to touch a blanket-bound baby
before nurses whisked him away.

She slept in fitful bursts,
the world surreal –
her image of mother and child forever shattered,
a large scar pulsing above her pubis.

Next morning she held him in her arms,
a perfect peach-skinned son
blessed with angelic features.
Plump; beautiful; ten fingers; ten toes.

Hungry, impatient at the breast,
she struggled, waiting for her milk to come in,
giving up on the fifth day to feed him a bottle.

She often lay, her firstborn
cradled in her arms
her whole being infused with love.
Her heart was like a thirsty flower
welcoming rain,
unaware of its capacity to bloom so fully
with such richness
until now.

Female Intuition

In a tree-lined Adelaide street
as the inhabitants slept,
the woman woke to absolute stillness,
the old house quiet.

Half-dozing, she lay,
an intuition of something amiss.
A sudden rush of nervous heartbeats,
urged her to check on her son.

Barefoot, she crossed a lamplit hallway
slipping head-first
around his bedroom door
(it was always left ajar),
eyes squinting in an effort to focus.

High ceiling,
picture rails like railway tracks
around the room's circumference,
her son's cot small against the wall
and him, sitting bolt upright,
a shadowy frozen silhouette,
cherubic curls framing a plump upturned face,
staring intently at the air vent
as light needled through its holes
in tiny golden spears.

Transfixed,
no sign of acknowledgement
although he must have heard her breathing there.

Gently, she laid him down,
the bottle in his mouth,
already sleepy.

She withdrew softly,
a strange sensation
settling as she returned to bed,
wondering at the oddness of it.

She caressed her pregnant belly
thoughts gone askew,
tiredness reclaiming her,
pondering if this baby
would be the daughter
she had already named.

Calamity or Care

Curtains drawn,
light pulsed at windows like hot hands.

The woman slid down the cool stone wall,
body slumped forwards in fatigue.
She watched her son sleep,
rounded O of cupid lips
forcing air to escape in tiny sighs;
brow damp from afternoon heat.

His beauty overwhelmed her
but today had been a challenge.

Something was not right.
She had tried to explain, but
no one wanted to believe.
Nanna said the boy was big for his age.
Her husband got angry;
there was nothing wrong with his son.

The local GP said
boys were, sometimes, slower to develop
(whatever the hell that meant!).
She thought of her son trapped in a roll of film
awaiting processing.
She felt inadequate; frustrated.
A tiny voice inside her head
kept warning of calamity,
but it spoke from some other dimension,
elusive, just out of reach.

What could it be?
What was its name?
Why did she feel so set upon?

Little Buddha

The mother's life was contained.
Domesticity,
constant care of baby, house and husband.
No friendships (all left behind in Tasmania)
but here, at least a mum, a sister,
some semblance of belonging.

The child gave such joy and happiness,
compensation for a bruised
and broken childhood,
a family fractured by dysfunction.

Sweet, her son, so sweet,
always content; playful
blue eyes shining with intelligence;
more often smiling than crying,
the apple of his nanna's eye.

He thrived on love and food and cuddles
but possessed an odd aloofness,
an inscrutability unusual in one so young –
hence the nickname 'Little Buddha'.

She was amazed
at how well he entertained himself
a preoccupation with his hands;
often fluttering them before his face
like two fledgling sparrows,
as if trying to disengage them from his body
so they could fly away.

Little Buddha's chubby face
soft and smooth as a satin doll,
free of earthly worry.

She mused about his future —
all the possibilities.

Corrugated Iron

The child sat, for all intentions
like a soft, cuddly toy,
plonked on his favourite beanbag
perfectly still, except for
little hands moving
in rhythmic, elegant fashion
turning the pages of his book
over and over and over.
Nothing else mattered.

He had a triangular toy that
spun on a base; a pyramid for
putting shapes into.
He would sit for ages spinning furiously,
watching it revolve,
crying out in heart-rending screams
if it was taken from him.

The mother felt uneasy,
as if some pressure was building,
gaining momentum,
somehow influencing their lives.

The boy spent large amounts of time
in the enclosed back garden
sometimes walking, sometimes running
the perimeter of fences –
corrugated iron for company.

Head held straight, and body rigid
he had a habit of
glancing sideways
out of the corner of narrowed eyes.

She called her husband to come and watch.
Isn't it strange?
It's nothing, he dismissed her fears,
just a little boy playing.

But what sort of play was this?

She'd take her son to playgroup
after the baby came.

That's all it was.

He needed friends his own age.
Why all this fretting and concern?
Couldn't she ever relax?
It made everyone miserable.

At Fifteen Months

The boy got sick after his vaccinations –
High fever, not turning his head,
lying still.
The doctor made a home visit
and, suspecting meningitis,
advised hospitalisation.

His mother cooked the evening meal,
insisting the family ate
before the trip into town.
She remembered the look in Nanna's eyes
as if to say,
What's going on inside your head?
Your son is sick.

While the boy had a spinal tap
she sat twisting her fingers; silent.
Don't panic, she told herself
He's young and strong. He'll be fine.
Detach. It's something you are good at.
Ignore your fear.

The boy was moved to a ward
and she remained at his side.
Her stepfather came one day with a gift.
A toy duck with a bright yellow bill
pink waistcoat and a floppy blue hat.
In the cot it sat.
The child looked at it curiously.
(Jemima Puddleduck lived with him for twenty years.)

The boy's diagnosis was changed to
severe gastroenteritis.
He slowly recovers
and is discharged from hospital, pale and thin.
The nightmare begins.

Baby Number Two

The boy seems withdrawn, not himself at all
as he lines his cars up in the hall.

His mother wakes one morning
breasts heavy, sore.
A pregnancy test confirms
what she already knows –
baby number two is on the way.

The boy's aloofness intensifies,
worrying her beyond belief.
She spends enormous amounts of time
reading to him.
Where have all his words gone?

She sings to him
(he always loved singing)
but he'd gaze past her
staring at the emptiness beyond
wide-eyed, silent.
It spooked her. Was something there?
Was the house haunted?

She showed him the old heavy pram
saying it was once his
and soon the new baby would be in it.
He only wanted to touch the wheels.

For his second Christmas
Nanna gave him a brightly coloured trike.
He turned it upside down
and spun the wheels relentlessly.

No one dared stop him.
It took too long to calm him down.

To Play, or How Not to Play

The boy collected garden snails,
placing them gently on the brick wall
by the back door.
If one moved out of line
he re-installed it to its former position.

Taps were a special love.
He would turn them on
many times a day
to watch water flow into the drain.
His mother turned them off,
he turned them on.

His father covered outside taps
with tin cans, holes drilled through,
tied on with string.

If Nanna came to visit
the boy would scream to go outside.
His mother ignored him, but he would lead her by the hand,
insistent, desperate,
becoming agitated unless she complied.
He would kneel to touch the car's wheels
or lie down to gaze at them lovingly.
A dangerous activity.

Power points,
switches, buttons, dials.
'On, off.' 'On, off.' 'On, off.'
All day long.

Spinning wheels; lining up sticks
flapping hands; constant screaming.
She mentioned these eccentricities
to her husband.

Don't be silly, he said.
Look at him. He's a healthy boy.

Once again, she voiced concerns
to her local GP
The boy sat sweetly on his mother's lap,
humming.
The doctor was impressed.

She asked the mother if she ever felt anxious.

Aha,
she believes I'm over-protective;
even slightly hysterical.
She took the boy home and packed
her maternity bag for the hospital.

I am becoming like my son, she thought.
To play, or how not to play?
That was the question.

A Son Foretold

The woman had a beautiful dream
in which her grandpa,
long deceased,
appeared to her.

He was in an amazing place,
face radiant,
surrounded by unearthly colour and light.
She told him she was pregnant
with her second child.
I know, he said. It's a boy.

She woke in the morning, euphoric,
enveloped in a peaceful calm.
Nothing her son did frustrated.

Her waters broke in the evening
and she rang Nanna
(who had not long ago gone home)
asking her
to take her grandson for the night.
This she did.

Her husband waited until midnight,
contractions getting stronger,
a thick towel beneath her in the car
on route to hospital.

Her son was born at 7.10 a.m.
Long elegant fingers,
black hair,
beautiful eyes.

She remembered Grandpa and his message.
The birth had gone well,
not the trauma of her first.

She gathered the new baby into her arms,
a monumental rush of deepest love
flowing from her into him.

She felt she had conquered
the highest mountain on earth.
She felt exhilarated and invincible.

Her husband stood, silent, unsure of what to say.
There had been unhappiness
before the birth.
Maybe this would bring them closer?
Maybe he would stay?

Sideways Glancing

The boy ignored his little brother.
The mother could not understand his indifference.
She wondered about him being deaf
but at the jiggling of car keys
he'd run to the door.

Newborn rituals settled,
she took the children to playgroup,
fulfilling her unspoken promise.
The boy preferred playing outdoors,
running the gauntlet of the fences
with that strange sideways glancing
she had first noticed at home.
She heard the other mothers muttering,
What's his problem?
Half a dozen visits, then she kept away.

One hot Adelaide morning
Nanna came to help,
driving them to nursing mothers.
In retrospect, thank goodness she had come!
Ceilings fans were cooling the rooms.
The boy took one look, screamed hideously
and sped outdoors.
Sister weighed and measured baby
to a chorus of wails from his terrified older brother.
Nanna tried all manner of things to calm him
but he wouldn't stop crying
until they were in the car.

She felt perplexed. How would she manage
next time on her own?
Why should a ceiling fan upset him so?

Little Arms Held Up

The baby did things so differently –
little arms held up for hugs,
walking at eight months
with beautiful balance and elegance,
high energy eclipsed
by even higher curiosity levels.
Green-flecked amber eyes,
sparkling with health and mischief,
following his brother;
trying to interact with him,
attempts to play met
with high-pitched screaming.

The baby, perplexed by constant rejection,
sometimes abandoned his attempts before
beginning them.
His mother worried at the ramifications.

Baby's logic was easy to work out.
He would ponder the situation
think, then turn away when his brother
was absorbed in a task.

Yet, still he persisted, the child with no fear,
while his brother seemed consumed by them,
crying at any intrusion.

She spoke with her husband,
who made light of her worries.

She understood his reluctance
to find fault with his firstborn.
Her own migrant father had done the same
with his firstborn,
longing for a son
not the girl fate had given him.
How odd, she thought,
these strangely evolving patterns
running through family histories in recurring themes.

Nanna became a willing supporter
driving her to see a specialist,
the boy compliant but uninterested in everything,
as if he was an observer from another world.

It was the beginning
of a new way of thinking,
a whole new world, as yet uncharted –
of wanting answers to questions,
of fear, despair, hopelessness
and helplessness;
of people who knew better,
of feeling angry and abandoned;
but most of all
the enormous, unflinching, untiring devotion
a mother has for her child
even when she knows their backs
are against the wall.

Wait and See

Referral to an early developmental childhood unit,
hospitalisation, ECG scans,
language and behaviour assessed and noted;
(the mother frightened)
endless questions asked by doctors
and then, the day she lost her son
and found him, almost supernaturally
replaced by another.
What did 'autistic' mean?
She had never heard this word before.

A new referral made to Autistic Children's Association,
home visit from a lovely guy
who spent hours watching the child, writing things down,
then booking a week for diagnostic tests.

Two days before the assessments
baby climbed onto a window ledge, fell
and broke his wrist; the mother consumed with guilt
for sleeping in and leaving her husband to cope
with two difficult kids.
Everything went from bad to worse –
both boys unsettled, baby miserable with pain
their mother miserable with anxious forebodings.

The boy's fingers flew to his ears a thousand times
to block out baby brother's crying.
What a mess! What a stinking, bloody mess!
The mother felt fear building like an enormous wave
waiting to engulf her,
to obliterate them all.

Stop it! she told herself. Wait and see.
Wait and see.
Wait and see.

Strange New World

The staff were welcoming, empathetic.
Protocols dispensed with, information gathered,
the business of assessment began.
They sat upstairs behind dark glass
in a long-windowed gallery.
The boy knew instinctively where to look –
bond to his mother strong.

He cried; he laughed.
They blew bubbles for and with him
and he forgot all his cares.
The diagnostic team worked steadily
through a barrage of tests,
the boy looking for his mother,
sobbing pitifully,
but then, resigned to it,
stacking blocks in colour, shape and size,
concentrating in a way he'd never done before.
When he couldn't continue,
they kindly let him, now and then,
release the pressure
by twirling pencils,
flapping hands, lining up toys
and making a beeline
for anything with wheels.

His mother discovered that autism
came from the Greek word *autos*
meaning to stand alone.
Her little son already had a Greek surname –
Now he had a Greek label as a bonus!

She left the gallery on a pretext
and stood outside smoking,
head aching and hot.

Anything was better than witnessing this thing,
this dysfunction,
this affliction that had befallen them.

Her heart was breaking.

The unspeakable pain she felt for her family
leeched into her very core.
It was the knowledge that they
were losing a son and brother
only to discover
that he was being reconfigured
by the professionals inside.
Father and son would have to adapt, somehow,
to a strange new world.

No maps to guide them,
no familiar galaxies or constellations,
just a void filled with dark matter.

She vowed that she would find a way.

But first she had to deal with grieving.

A Pyramid of Three

The mother cried a lot;
mainly in the shower.
Her husband started a part-time job
washing dishes
in a posh North Adelaide restaurant.

She spent quiet evenings with the boys,
nightly rituals of moon-gazing
singing by the jacarandas;
rocking the baby to sleep; his sweet warm smell
a soothing balm –
a pyramid of three,
the boys at each corner of its base
with her balanced delicately on its apex,
mental strength returning,
a renewal of purpose,
Eastern European determination kicking in.

Her life was removed from all things
except mothering and wifely duties,
a shift to government housing,
secure accommodation
closer to mum; feeling connected,
attaining a driver's licence (at 32!),
making progress with the boys.

She watched and learnt a lot from the boy's
early intervention teachers.
She modified, trialled, reinforced,
was consistent.
It was paying dividends,
but her husband was unsettled, maybe feeling left out,
flitting back and forth to Melbourne,
reconnecting to family and friends
as he sailed the choppy wake
of his son's little boat
widening in ever-growing ripples.

Pressure Builds

The mother worried for her younger boy;
he had terrible nightmares,
rousing the house with his screams,
eyes rolling back in their orbits,
disoriented, babbling.
'Night terrors,' said the experts.
Confusion and rejection, she thought.
Ours is not a normal family;
the rules are different for him –
scared of his brother's odd behaviour.

She tried to compensate while his brother
was at early intervention programs.
She tried to explain in simple terms,
but he would look away, pretending not to hear.

Special outings. Cooking together.
Offering comfort and reassurance.
It seemed that he had lost his equilibrium,
lost his footing on the pyramid,
and as he tried to make sense of things
in front of him, there was the endless desert of his brother –
and when he thought he'd found some clue
to the mystery of his brother's world,
it slipped from his reach like a mirage.

Her little son could not deal with the pain.
Silent, angry and withdrawn,
it was a sign of things to come.
He began slamming doors,
fear turned to violence
and he often hurt himself in the process.

Other People

Other people's lives
seemed to flow
in a natural order of progression,
things falling into place as they should –
children adapting smoothly to the many changes
in their life;
accepting, trusting, comprehending,
kindy, preschool, primary school.
But for the boy it needed huge orchestration,
teams of people, building layer upon layer,
networks needed
connecting A to B and C to D –
like some covert operation –
frightening in a way
because at its essence
the unknown hovered.
How could one define what was always best?
The child was too tiny to have a voice.

The mother agonised.
So many opposing points of view.
Normal school? Special school?
Attention to detail vital,
hours of attendance to be negotiated,
teacher-training, in-service,
autism so different to
the majority of kids with special needs.

She drank too much,
often staggering to bed
too pissed to care.
It was all too hard; her husband had no words of wisdom,
his own needs sometimes complex, introverted,
leaving her in a whirl of anxiety,
unsure of decisions; not wanting fury rained upon her
if it all fell in a heap.

She feared the judgement of family and friends.
She feared failing her son.
She was frightened of making mistakes
and having to start all over again.

She needed to get back to basics.
This was about her child.
A third of her life had already passed;
his was barely started.

Have a drink, she chided herself,
not the whole bloody bottle!
History is not repeating itself.
Try to believe.

Break the hoodoo.

Bring it to its knees.

Monologue of the Self

For a boy who hardly spoke,
he spent most days
in an endless monologue of the self.

'Mum, green eyes,
Bubby, brown-yellow eyes,
Dad, green eyes,
Nanna, green eyes,' and so on and so forth,
of all the people in his life.
And if it wasn't words
it was continual humming
like a small train idling at the station,
or soulful little songs like
'Ah…wee wee wee, ah…oh oh oh.'
Could he be the reincarnation of a Sioux?

His bedroom a universe, where he sat
for hours
cross-legged before a cassette player
listening to music; playing with the buttons,
re-winding, stopping, fast-forwarding,
until it sounded almost
like a symphony of clicks; of singing whales
sounding out messages
making sense of the world.

The mother would stand quietly at the door
amazed at his absorption in it;
the oneness with all he did –
an extraordinary ability to go into himself.

Experts called it self-stimulatory behaviour,
obsessional; fixated.
The mother saw a child who had purpose,
was driven,
qualities of strength, focus and patience,
of trying to construct order out of chaos.

There had to be a key.

She must watch him carefully,
encourage him
in all his interests.

One day the monologue
would become a dialogue.
He would find another way –
but it had to be his own.

His hand must be the one
to open the door.

Irrational Fears

It was cruel for all the family.
So many fears; so much screaming.

In the house with jacaranda trees
lilac flowers and shining stars
it had been lawnmowers
fan heaters, ceiling fans
his brother's insistence at play,
other children near him,
the boy collapsing into heart-rending sobs
terror-stricken and shaking,
his mother unable to comfort him.

In the new house
he wouldn't eat in the kitchen
(sitting at a small table in the hallway
like an unwanted orphan)
or go into the bathroom
because of exhaust fans.

He would stand in the doorway
transfixed with fear, screaming
'Off!' 'Off!' 'Off!' 'Off!'
Little brother could not understand
and was afraid as well.

A fear of bodily motions;
refusing to toilet
especially at other people's houses,
and as a consequence
painful bowel movements.
She discovered singing in the toilet
at the tops of their voices
could be distracting and useful –
a relaxed child lets go!

Obsessive chatter; 'fans, fans, fans' –
as if they had come to earth
to take control of human beings
and change world order.

A fear of dogs, all dogs
large or small,
fingers flying to his ears
in case they barked.
His mother knew the sound must
shoot into his head like a bullet –
loud; reverberating and painful.

Irrational fears halt learning;
a desensitisation program devised
around his fan phobia
and the boy looks like he'll die of trauma,
but weeks and months later
he can switch those devilish contraptions
on and off himself,
a strange sideways glancing,
but do-able; a done deal,
terror overcome, defeated and removed,
four people at the kitchen table
to share a meal –

a family once again.

Irrational Loves

Digging holes in the kindy sandpit
and at the beach,
constructing pipes and drainage systems
for water to be poured into
from a hose, a bucket,
a tap, any tap – all the taps! –
in an endless stream.

If the boy could get to water
he was a happy chappy,
a true Aquarian,
a problem habit in Adelaide summers,
water precious,
outside taps covered with empty tins
holes drilled through
tied tight with string.

Collecting twigs for spinning,
an especially favoured love,
and the use of objects to line up shadows
in mathematical precision.
He could tell the time without
ever needing a clock.
What artistry and creativeness!

Plump hands fluttering
like leaves in a breeze
or sparrows darting in the sky –
restless fingers, as if needing to sense
the world around him with their tips –

Could these be a form of human antennae?

He enjoyed the sound of his voice
and loved producing unusual vocal vibrations.

Cassette tapes, lovingly turned
over and over
placed in the player; removed;
the process repeated endlessly
until either exhausted or distracted from the task.

TDK. No other brand acceptable!

On wet days
windscreen wiping in the car,
arms bent at angles, perfect timing
to the sweep of blades;
remarkable mimicry
produced from pouting lips –
soft whooshing sounds of rain and rubber on glass.

A next-door neighbour said the child
did perfect crow imitations
and cooed exactly like the pigeons kept in the backyard.

An irrational love of M&Ms
and a total fixation with the letter M
like Mitsubishi –
this love will last a lifetime, his mother thinks.

Chocolate is everywhere
in many forms
but only M&Ms will do.

An adult now,
he often makes this statement,
'I think I need energy'
before setting off to purchase
his favourite confectionery.

And he drives a Mitsubishi car.

Rational Loves

The Mitsubishi car logo – a triple diamond;
diamonds were this boy's best friend.
In later life this love transformed
like many a young man growing up
into the purchase of a first car
saved for over many months
and paid for in cash.
The car's badge, with its three red triangles
still holds a place in his heart.

The mother intuits this at a fundamental level
because his mouth trembles with pleasure
each time he washes it,
eyes flickering over the logo with reverence;
a quiet, inward satisfaction.

A passion for the functions and methodology
of all life on earth,
diverse interests, like biology, astronomy,
tectonic plates, the human embryo,
habits of cats, their colours, size and markings.
Trains; the TGV of France
and bullet trains of Japan.
Planes and airports, architecture, house design
(a dream of designing his own one day).
Patterns and sounds in music, especially unusual instruments
like the shamisen, cimbalom, taiko drums or bagpipes.
A plan drawn out of his own symphony orchestra
revised occasionally into new and revolutionary forms.
Patterns and percentages of numbers.
Photography.

A deep love of the night sky;
intricate knowledge of star systems and planets,
exact degrees to horizons known; indeed
the order of such things essential to well-being;
structure a constant in his life, such as
phases of the moon marking out the days of every month.

A love
a true desire
to embrace and understand the cosmos,
a final wish to have his ashes
catapulted into deep space aboard a rocket.

A strong belief that the future
of our planet is out there –
a true visionary.

A love for his own inner space
so vital to health and balance;
relishing a place of safety and creativity.

A love for privacy;
somewhere to think and dream
and maybe agonise at the hardness of it all
(especially people; how hard are they?)
but mostly

a place for him to be his 'self',
a room of his own
where he can speak the words out loud
so that their meaning is real,
so that his thoughts can live.

Thinking in New Ways

The boy's first day of school
created deep anguish in his mother's heart.
Would he cope without her?
Would he understand what was needed
from him by others?
She tried to remember all the positives
about the school.
It was caring; small; the principal eager,
willing to include;
its Roman Catholicism and social justice values
she had experienced herself
and found not perfect, but responsive
to the human condition in all its states.
She committed her son into their hands –
an act based on trust.

Months of half-days, early pick-ups,
Autistic Children's Association teachers
worth their weight in gold,
school staff patient, professional,
learning that this student's needs were not the same
as other kids with special needs;
teachers re-evaluating, assessing, adapting –
willing to think in new ways.

Younger brother started school the following year
and settled in well,
both boys leaving together in the mornings
happy, singing in the car –
hugs and kisses at the gate.

The woman felt, in the happy smiles
of the boy's classmates,
a gradual connection to other mums,
an acceptance and open-heartedness.
She found new friends.

Forward Planning

Years passed, as years do.
The woman became involved in many aspects of the school,
volunteering time and effort,
hoping it would make a difference to those
who dealt with her son.

It was a form of gratitude.
A way of thanking them. Her contribution.

Many hours every month
spent in forward planning,
communication flowing,
vigilance imperative.
The boy progressed and learnt.
There were certain topics he enjoyed,
became obsessive about,
accumulating enormous knowledge.

Sometimes he refused to do set work,
wanting to make tiny replicas of light bulbs
or to draw the human embryo
in various stages of development.
Such beautiful creations!
Teachers were sometimes puzzled,
unsure of how to lure him back
into the fold.

He was like a bird flying above the earth
searching for a place to land,
looking for a tree with strong branches
to support and hold him up,
his days an agony of sensory overload
and anxious existing,
personal safety found in fixations and rituals
because the world so often terrified and confused.

Stress Gains Momentum

The signs, at first, were confusing.
Recurring headaches, bouts of lethargy,
loud self-talk at home; louder at school.
Vibrating noises an avoidance tactic
hoping for removal from the classroom
to a blissful, secluded time out,
and at home, to his bedroom.

The mother found a note
in her son's communication booklet
written to his teacher.

5.06.1992
'Problems'
'i tried to say sorry
but you would not let me
will you let me say sorry plese
on Tuesday and no TIME OUT
with the heddmaster
i tried very very
hard and tried
to not swer
i tried to work
and do graph
i wont be steperd
those boys
shout out my
name long ago
but now I will
have help of
work from you

that girl always says
she gowing to
tell heddmaster

I dont care if I have
workroom time out because
all those silly things I say
i should say sorry
id never ever call you names
i should reply you to let me
say sorry
i will be very nice to you
and you could be very nice to me
those people who shouted out
my name loudley
they can say sorry
and remind for that boy to say
sorry
BE NICE PLEASE
write back'

The mother showed this to the teacher
(what a strange disquieting smile she possessed!)
and asked about the issues her son had raised.
He was asking for help and forgiveness.
He had an utter horror of anyone misusing his name
and this was self-evident from the note.
He was saying sorry to his teacher for being upset.

He was feeling intimidated by other students.
The mother wanted to ease his confusion
but this could not happen
until she understood what lay beneath.

Teasing and Tantrums

The boy had a classmate, a round-faced girl,
who said she was his friend.
She moved houses a lot
and gave him a different phone number every day
with which to call her.

The phone numbers belonged to other students
and he became upset and confused
when he rang and she wasn't there.

She insisted the next day at school
the number she was giving him
was the 'real' one.
After all, she was his friend.

She thrived on power
and tormenting one less able.
She came from a well-known Adelaide family
whose father was going places.
She was untouchable, and the system
would protect her at the boy's expense.
His sacrifice would go unnoticed.
Who would care about one little boy?

The girl whispered that she would tell on him
and have him sent to the principal's office.
The boy would become distraught; he had done nothing wrong
and lacked the skills to explain his dilemma.

He absconded from school twice,
his absence unnoticed for hours.
How derelict was the school in protecting him?
They did not bother to inform his mother.

In the name of Christ, shame.
Shame, shame, shame.
Gather the little children in thy care.

Collision Course

It was the boy's last year at primary school
and his mother felt everything disintegrating –
five years of hard work
heading towards a collision course.

The taunting rocketed to new levels
and stirred revolt deep within the boy.
Not one to attack,
he screamed, yelled and swore
in an effort to fend off his oppressor.
Suspension after suspension
saw more time spent at home
than at school.

What was going so wrong?
School and staff had ample training and input
about autism and its management,
strategies and knowledge learnt over the years.

Of all the students there was only one
who tormented and targeted him.
His mother asked for a meeting with the girl's family
to resolve the issue of bullying,
to help the children move forward,
but the Principal refused her request.

Why was the Principal so immovable?
Couldn't she see the injustice?
She lacked clarity, and as a consequence
all fairness had been stripped away.

Burnt at the Stake

The mother went unexpectedly one afternoon
to collect her son early,
concerns heightened
at an increase in time outs.

'Me good boy.' 'Time out office.'

She wondered if this was acting
as a reinforcer and complicating matters.

She arrived to find him
exactly in the place he hated most
asleep on the floor of the principal's office
like a stray dog,
the Catholic Education Vision Statement
dissolving before her eyes.
He was fatigued, hot, thirsty
frightened and alone – a bucket near his head
to catch his vomit.

Upset, fearful and perplexed
she took him home.
What to do for the best?
He was like Joan of Arc in a child's body,
a scapegoat to be burnt at the stake,
his needs ignored, his rights of little consequence.

Who to trust or turn to?

Soon this question would be answered
in a chorus of disbelief,
the sacrifice complete.

Five is a Magical Number

It was the fifth month of the last year –
year five, before the boy's Tier II education would begin.
There was a regular student disability review
focusing on his transition to college,
a subject of great importance
during the previous twelve months –
not one concern raised about threatening behaviours
or inability to manage his needs.

The following day, 25 May,
saw the boy lunge at a staff member
as the Principal steered him on route to her office
for the inevitable time out.
'Lunge' was to become her word of the year
as the boy's world spiralled into panic and high anxiety,
unable to cope with impossible demands
and unrealistic expectations.
The bully's taunts increased unabated.

On 15 June the Principal rang
at 7.30 p.m. Unusual, to say the least.
She demanded an urgent meeting be attended
the following day. Not could you, or would you?
Just do it! Keep your son at home!
The mother asked what the meeting was about
but she refused to explain.
It was a long, wakeful night!

Next morning the parents arrived
to a solemn, foreboding welcome at the school gate
and were directed to its chapel –
the Principal and two CEO* Special Education Officers
were waiting for them to take their seats –
five chairs set in a circle.
It was said in thirty seconds.
Their son was being expelled.

* CEO: Catholic Education Office

Taking it to the Next Level

The family were in deepest shock.
In the three weeks
since the boy's last suspension
and subsequent expulsion
his mother had attended seven long meetings
trying to resolve matters.
At the Principal's request, another in-service
for staff had taken place.
At its conclusion
it was agreed all staff implement
the behaviour modification program devised
until the end of June.
The boy was expelled on 16 June.

He blamed the bully for his misfortune,
their problems not worked through,
neither child helped by the school to find some resolution.
How sad for the children!

Exclusion from school
meant loss of routines, friendships
and no education.
For the mother and her family
it created emotional pain and heartache,
years of hard work swept away.

A week after the expulsion
the Principal sent a letter to every family of the school
(a unilateral decision)
stating the boy was a danger to all the children.
Her best friend came one day,
grim-faced and disgusted,
bearing a letter
handed to her after school
by her young daughter.

The family were astonished by the letter.
Nothing could be further from the truth.

Not one member of the school staff
having claimed so passionately
to love this child in Christ's name,
made a visit to the house
or rang to speak with the child
to ask him how he was.

It was as if the family had never existed.

Suffer the Little Children

The boy's obsessions worsened,
old fixations returning;
hours spent spinning objects,
increased noisiness and difficulty sleeping.

His friends at school missed him.
His mother was told
how the children watched, tearfully,
as his things were cleared out
and removed from the classroom,
no explanations given.

The school community rose up in one voice.
Letters written; sincere and sensitive
missals of support;
visits made to CEO head office
demanding the child's reinstatement,
and then dramatically,
a removal of their children in protest
for days,
meeting up with the boy at a local park,
sharing lunch and fun and games,
a photo taken (what a wonderful souvenir!),
his mother's heart infused forever
with the loving kindness of the families
and their belief that he belonged.

Looking For Justice

Eight long months passed.
The parents continued to press
for answers to their questions,
for some minuscule acknowledgement
of their family's collective hurt and anguish
and for their son's reputation to be reinstated.

The mother and her advocates met
with the Director of the CEO.
He discussed his own illness and retirement
while she sat in horror,
her complaints glossed over,
no obvious awareness of the impact on her family's life.

At the heart of this
was a child, constantly asking
when he could go back to school.
To this end an Adelaide lawyer,
wanting to find a better way.
took on their case with gusto,
his own children in the Roman Catholic system,
a system, he realised,
sadly lacking the strength to direct
that a wrong should be righted.

The mother was yet to learn of the endless shenanigans
and dirty tricks employed by CEO lawyers.

One hot summer night,
immense pressure escalating,
she snapped, screaming at the children,
yelling at her husband,
frustration and rage boiling over,
threw a few things in a bag,
and absconded from her family for days.

Alone and close to breaking point,
pent-up feelings released themselves.
Uncontrollable bouts of weeping,
hours of sleeping,
more weeping,
a gradual calming down,
emotional upheaval subsiding,
she rang her husband on the fourth day
to come and take her home.

He was more worried than angry.

He understood that something
cataclysmic had taken place;
a turning point.

The family had suffered enough.
Puzzled by their mother's unusual absence
they watched her every move,
relief showing in their faces,
both boys clingy.

She would never leave her family again.

Marvellous Marion Primary School

Many people,
too many to name on this page,
were instrumental
in helping the boy return
to his local public school, Marion Primary –
ten minutes from home.

This school understood
the challenge before them,
expending much effort, time and planning
for his re-entry into education in 1994.
The class teacher worked hard
in restoring his new student's broken image.
A traumatised and damaged little boy!

His mother continued, resolute
upon the legal pathway,
two things foremost in her mind;
the first, now unachievable –
her son's reinstatement in the Roman Catholic system
impracticable over the passage of time –
but the second, an apology,
was a matter she would pursue
for the horrid treatment they had received;
for the lies and wicked innuendos
the Principal told the local priest
after he made a plea on the boy's behalf.

The Principal had demonised her son,
an innocent child.
For this, there had to be resolution.
Nothing less than an apology would suffice.

Legal Matters

Months rolled by.
The boy was doing relatively well,
his brother not so well.
The mother removed him from his school
and sent him to
another government school.
Both boys had quit the Roman Catholic system,
too much damage done to them –
the repercussions dogged her family for years.

Legal matters
took a life of their own
as the CEO continued to remain
intransigent, uncooperative, obstinate –
a nightmare without end; like pulling teeth!

And yet the 1991 SACCS* Student Behaviour Policy R-12
stated clearly that responsibilities for principals were
'to ensure that the Gospel values of justice,
reconciliation and respect for human dignity
are modelled and supported in a school environment
which recognises the unique presence of God in all people.'

Furthermore, the policy statement on page 2 claimed,
'Schools base behaviour management processes
upon the values of justice and reconciliation
with an explicit respect for human dignity.'

And adding insult to injury, that
'Schools develop a system or rights…
in an atmosphere of love, hope, joy and faith.
This development is fostered by cooperative
negotiation between staff, students and families.'

No more fancy words! Enough was enough.
Let them practise what they preached.

* SACCS: South Australian Commission for Catholic Schools

No More Empty Words

No more empty words.
No more pretending.
The boy either existed, a child of God,
or he did not!

His needs were the same as every human being;
to have opportunities to learn,
to create, to be happy
and to dance in the sun.

As 1994 drew to an end
the CEO and his mother
were still locked in combat.
The Human Rights and Equal Opportunity Commission
took up her complaint,
lawyers and an army of believers
pushed for resolution,
working hard
not just for the boy and his family
but for all the families of his former school,
demanding justice for their children's friend,
their support unwavering.

Through her despair and anger
she felt sustained, uplifted by those families,
a deep gratitude and mutual love;
but in spite of this outpouring of parental support
an emptiness had formed,
an aversion to a geographical place
that made her physically unwell and emotionally distressed.

She wanted to return to Tasmania,
her childhood island home,
but was not yet sure of how or when.

She could not live in Adelaide any more.

The Hearing

Peter was an exemplary lawyer.
He knew his craft and ran with it
like a thoroughbred to the line.
He pummelled the table, neck stretched forward
steel-grey mane of hair swept back
framing an animated, impassioned face.

Elegant hands held tight
the reins of righteousness,
eyes focused on the prize.

All through that long morning
his words rose and fell in measured strides,
truths emanating from his lips like songs.

The parents heeded his counsel
as the battle raged,
their child's young life and reputation
argued and fought for,
no turning back, their resolve strong.

The Principal never showed.
A principal with no principles,
her absence simply reinforced
her lacklustre attitude to the family
she'd wronged.
CEO officials sat with their legal team
tight-lipped
refusing to apologise,
blaming the mother for their uncooperative stance.

Eyes downcast, she smiled sadly.
Peter shot back at them
words fired like bullets from a gun.

She took the legal path, he bellowed,
after trying everything in her power
to resolve matters in a dignified manner.

Thus it continued until
a midday break when ranks re-formed
to face each other across the wide table.
It felt like gazing at the mountains of the moon.

Ex gratia payments offered
(blood money given from the goodness
of their Christian hearts!)
and her refusal, given swiftly.

More debate; more offers –
the parents rejecting every one,
the winter day fading,
light leaking from the sky like a bleeding heart.

She turned to Peter, angry, seeking resolution
from the drawn-out dismal day.
She said,
Tell them we only ever wanted
to hear them say they were sorry.
Tell them we don't want their money.
Tell them to apologise to our son and to us.
Go to hell!

He negotiated exactly what she asked for,
the CEO paying for their legal costs,
the parents satisfied,
leaving with five lines on a piece of paper
and a hole in their hearts
left by twenty-four months of hurt, humiliation
and total disregard
for the irreparable damage
done to their little boy.

To this very day
he still talks about what happened to him.

Explorations

The mother knew the time had come
for explorations,
returning briefly to her island home,
welcomed by her brother and his partner
where four days were spent
visiting schools on the north-west coast
meeting special education personnel
and principals, formulating a possible transition
for the boys into a school.
A school was found;
the principal, Mike, a man of vision
prepared to think flexibly,
would play a pivotal role in their high school years,
his extraordinary insight and commitment a rare jewel.

Back in Adelaide, her mind was set,
decisions made;
the family prepared for the eventual move,
her sons unsure of the unknown
but, being young, the choice made for them.

Mountains of work to be done,
boxes packed, garage sale,
travel arrangements organised.
The departure day arrived.
Farewells to mother, sister, brother,
the hardest goodbye to nephew, little Ed
(such sadness; she adored him)
left to grow without his cousins;
farewells to friends and supporters,
the parting bitter-sweet,
so many loving relationships left behind.

It all fell away from her, no turning back,
a heart in mourning for those so loved
but in her mind she acknowledged what she must do
to ensure its very survival.

New Beginnings

The father drove a hired truck to Melbourne
chock-full with their belongings.
His wife, the boys and cat
followed by car.
A night sailing across Bass Strait
to a bright, cold morning,
light winging through the air
in a shimmering benediction.

It was November 1st 1995 –
five months since the hearing;
a new way of living and adapting had begun.

Her brother met them at Devonport,
escorting them to the house he'd found,
a sturdy federation red-brick structure
looking out across a sweeping foreshore park,
ocean glittering beyond it
beneath a blue cloud-strewn sky.

Her first night was restless;
different sounds awoke her,
waves thudding to the beach,
seagulls calling to each other,
plovers screeching in the darkness,
diving sentinels on wings.

She woke early, made coffee
and sat on the front veranda
overwhelmed with fatigue, but happy.
Seabirds soared in a sunrise sky,
underbellies tinted peach and rose,
sparkling waves jostled for position at the horizon's edge,
and her heart lifted up.
Tom the cat ecstatic;
a lap on which to purr.

Hope Renewed

The years that followed
witnessed challenges beyond belief.
The woman paid a price for isolation
but with such stunning beauty
laid out at her door,
ever-changing ocean with its curving bays and inlets,
patchwork farmland, sweeping hills,
wilderness, rivers, waterfalls pouring over stone,
and a green so green
it sprouted fields of flowers in her heart.
This would evolve into a crucible for feelings
forged from the sacred moments
only nature, stillness and silence can bequeath.

Sunshine, sea and starry nights offered peace.
From this a gradual healing flowed,
at first a tiny trickle meandering timidly,
forming tributaries, ideas growing,
building into rivers of thought,
motivating fingers to pen,
words to paper,
her writer's soul burst open
in a harvest of new-found creativity,
her journey worth the price,
its end a little slice of paradise,
strength and hope renewed.

Galactic Movements

The woman's son graduated
from high school in his eighteenth year.
Four years on, since the move from Adelaide,
new skills emerged
that serve him to this very day.

His teenage years were traumatic, tortured,
confused and lonely,
but he acknowledged in his twenties
that no one escapes those years unscathed.

Resilience, growing maturity,
a case manager who cared,
saw him exposed to new experiences and learning.
He moved forwards, slowly and steadily,
like the spiralling arm of a huge galaxy.

Music composition, computer graphics and design,
film making, recording studio training,
attaining a drivers licence and independence
counterbalanced his social isolation,
depressions and anxieties.

He learnt to walk the walk
even though he often couldn't understand the talk.

Living by Bass Strait
so close to sky and sea
saw a passionate interest in astronomy,
moon-rises and moon-sets
in heavenly patterns,
degrees to the horizon of stars and constellations,
the stability of facts and figures.
These imparted wonder, meaning and great joy.

A cheeky, fun-loving person emerged,
unafraid of cameras and film makers,
inspired by his hero, Sacha Baron Cohen,
and other comic actors,
Jim Carrey, Rowan Atkinson –
a perfect mimic,
a memory for whole movie scripts;
a stint at an acting career,
his movies shown at local cinemas,
his mother amazed at his boldness on the huge screen.

Those who recognised his abilities
helped expand his creative journey
continuing their mentorship in many ways.
Acceptance, tolerance, a fair go
gave him pride in his achievements.

He knew how good it felt
to be just one of the guys.

Continuum

The great sea of life
carried the young man onwards
its currents and tides
eddies and whirlpools
depositing him on near and far away shores.

He wrote a book about his life,
formed his own truths and ethics,
an honest, brave, good citizen,
proud son of his nation.

His family
learnt lessons on belonging,
on hatred and prejudice,
on exclusion and ignorance –
what it is to deal with difference
and how people see this difference.
Life was full of hardship
but when the sweetness came
it could be nothing else but sweetness.

Wider family, good people and friends
balanced all the dark times,
sorrows and joys side by side,
as is the way of each and every life.

The mother's real happiness was to see her sons
live out their passions,
to be honest, caring men –
her love stored in their hearts
a legacy to hold for all time.

Autist – Moon Searcher

We carry images deep inside us
until the day we die
like holy icons
with hinged doors closed.
Sometimes we open them,
colours vivid in the light,
and bless the day
that we were born with eyes.

For the woman, it would be an image
always treasured –
a moment held outside
the bonds of time.

Occasionally she'd glance at her son
as mothers often do;
his face would hold a certain look –
a reverence, a fascination,
maybe a thought, or a thing he saw –
and a memory flashed,
a resurrection
of a moment cradled in her mind;
it represented a duality,
the human and divine.

She recalled a summer night
in the old house near the sea,

the young man standing by the tea-tree
in the garden, silently.

Unaware of her, he scanned the sky,
his face serene,
sunset flooding him
like a Phidias marble in a temple
transformed into a living flame,
gazing upwards intently
as if the whole earth had slipped away,
searching for the crescent moon.

There was such stillness in that moment
swathed in goldish-tangerine,
time passing slowly –
then a tiny shift of bottom lip
a double-eyelash blink,
the prize was found,
the sky revealed its order for him
connecting him to place and time.

He needed this,
his marker of existence,
more than anyone could ever understand.

He smiled,
and let the night draw softly in.

www.ingramcontent.com/pod-product-compliance
Lightning Source LLC
Chambersburg PA
CBHW062147100526
44589CB00014B/1715